Tears of a Child's Innocence

Tears of a Child's Innocence

A STORY ABOUT TRUTH FORSAKEN

LaDonna W. Smith

ISBN:978-1-7374468-0-4

Publisher: LaDonna Smith
Publisher Consultant:

SP

SOPHISTICATED
P R E S S

Manufactured in the United States of America

Acknowledgments

First and foremost, I thank God who is the head of my life. He is the Father, Son, and Sweet Holy Spirit; He saved me and allowed me to write this book.

I want to thank my mother for giving me life; I love her very much. I know being a single mother was very hard. Because of my childhood, I am stronger and wiser.

My daughter, Latoya Wingate, God has a crown with your name on it. You are a precious jewel. Through my sickness and surgeries, you were right by my side,

My son, Chad Gingles, I love you. You are very special; you are my firstborn child. Son, words can not express the love I have for you and your sister.

To my siblings, I love you all.

To my editor, Lady Rachel Brown. I can go on and on. Words can't express my gratitude or thanks for everything you have done for me.

Pastor Johnny Brown, thank you for being an awesome leader. You are setting an example as a kingdom builder for the Lord.

Dedications

My granddaughter, Layla Bean, I am so grateful to God for blessing me with you. You are a beautiful miracle; you changed my life for the better.

I would like to recognize a few people that have impacted my life:

My best friend, Nanette Galmon. I appreciate your sisterly love for over 30 years.

My god brother, O'Nicklas Lindsey, I love you...

Mother Rosalind Morrison, much love to you...

Mrs. Jane McLean, I extend a special thank you to you and your family. I know God sent me an angel here on earth. After your son, my friend, Jason McLean passed away. I was grateful to have met such an amazing soul,

Thank you Mrs. Jane for your love and support.

The late Mamie Wilson, a beautiful angel...

Lib Bynum, my sweet aunt, your love was so beautiful. You helped me through my pain.

Jackie Johnson, thank you for your love and support. I love you. You are my friend.

Contents

Introduction

I've always felt there was a need to tell my story, not to make anyone feel bad or to embarrass any of my family. Many years have gone by, and God has given me the strength to free the little girl inside of me. After going through counseling after counseling, I always ended up back in the same place, not healed. Finally, I am at a place where I am striving for wholeness. I want to help show many other little girls that God can fix and mend their brokenness. I have learned to love again and truly forgive everyone who has abused, lied to, hurt, and betrayed me. All the glory belongs to God. Without Him, there would be no book or stories to tell. He deserves the highest praise.

As I was writing this book, I decided to change the characters' names. Writing this book took me back to so much pain filled with restless nights and countless nightmares. I blocked many of my experiences out of my mind for so many years. Now, I am free and ready to tell my story.

To tell my story, I had to pray and fast because I had to relive so many bad and hurtful scenes in my head. God knows I have shed many tears, but it was all a part of the process. I still remember the painful words spoken to me as a child. "Nessa, you are worthless." Nessa, the main character who conveys my life, reflects on the pain she experienced as a child.

CHAPTER 1

A Little Girl Within Me

Nessa was a shy girl; she was aware of the obstacles surrounding her life. She found happiness in solitude because she didn't want to explain her life situations to others. Growing up at Simon Creek Baptist Church was good; however, she couldn't find her way to a normal life because of the pain, rejection, and abuse. She desperately wanted the church to be the remedy to all of her problems. She was always in the church because her mother believed she should be there. Nessa's mother, Francis, was a very hard worker and a great mother. She worked hard to provide for her family. She was strict and very protective. They went to Sunday school and morning service every Sunday. She didn't send them, but she took them. Francis was a Sunday school teacher; she kept her children busy working in the church.

As a child, Nessa was a momma's girl. She would eat popsicles from her mother's freezer with her siblings, and she would take cookies out of the jar without her mother's permission. She would always lie to her mom and say that her siblings ate the cookies and popsicles. She was a child; children always told white lies. Francis knew Nessa was guilty. Every mother knows when her child is lying; I think it is just a mother's intuition. Nessa never wanted her mother to be mad at her. She loved her mother, but she would do crazy things. For example,

Nessa would say she didn't eat the popsicle, but her tongue was the color of the popsicle. Sometimes, she would get punished, and sometimes she wouldn't.

When Francis' new boyfriend, Ray, came into her life, Nessa's life changed forever. Nessa watched her mother's behavior change. She no longer spent time with her children. Francis shared with her boyfriend that Nessa was a liar. Young children will sometimes stretch the truth, but a mother should never label a child as a liar to her boyfriend or anyone for that matter. Nessa still remembers the vivid conversations between Francis and her best friend. "Nessa always gets into everything, " her mother replied. She is always getting whoopings." Ray would sit and listen to the conversations. Ray seemed to be a nice guy at first; however, he changed over time. Nessa and her family lived in government housing, which assisted struggling mothers. At the time, they were very happy. They didn't have a lot of money, but they had a lot of love. Nessa and her mother had a close bond, but the bond changed when she labeled her as a liar. Nessa didn't tell habitual lies for her mother to label her as a liar. Ray used her mother's label to his benefit. As Nessa reflects on her life, she believes her mother's boyfriend saw a lady with kids (majority girls) and wanted to be a part of their world. He started to take them to the county fair, Myrtle Beach, and on small vacations during Spring and Summer breaks. He wanted to get his foot in the door because he knew they never went out of Gastonia. Ray appealed to their vulnerabilities and curiosities. Nessa was a momma's girl, and she was very shy. When Francis didn't have male friends over, Nessa would sleep with her. When Ray would spend the night, Nessa would have a bad feeling because of the way he undressed her with his eyes. Ray would come over regularly to spend time with Francis. Later, Francis got sick. Before her surgery, Ray would come over and spend the night with Francis. Nessa and her big sister, Michelle, were sleeping in the same room with twin beds. In the middle of the night, Ray came into the room. Nessa woke up, and Michelle was asleep. He put his finger over his mouth for Nessa not to scream. Being a child, she was scared; he put his hands all over her body. Then, he told her he would kill her mother if she told the truth. Then he said, "you are a liar anyway. " Nessa was shattered.

After Francis had surgery Ray was back and forth from his place to Francis' house watching the kids while she was in the hospital for a few days. Nessa stayed out of his way. She was scared because she didn't know what his next move would be. When Francis came home, she noticed plates and cups were missing. Ray told her that they were breaking the plates or giving them away. He reminded Francis that Nessa lied about things. When Francis got well, she whooped Nessa and Michelle for the missing items. Ray told Francis that they broke the dishes, so they wouldn't have to wash them. As a child, Nessa always believed Ray had something to do with the missing items. She just couldn't prove it. As Francis was getting better, they started missing blankets, sheets, and pillowcases. The sisters were hurt and confused, being so young. They didn't understand why all these things were happening. Ray had their mother exactly where he wanted her. Later, he convinced Francis to move in with him, so he could have control. I still remember her voice: " We must stay with Ray." When she told her kids, they were not happy. She explained how his house was better than theirs. Not true, Ray's place was the worst. Nessa knew her life was going to be a living hell. She watched her life decline; she learned quickly that love is so blind. While living in Ray's house, they had no friends, no visits, and endured more beatings. Francis' items continued to go missing from the house. Nessa continued to experience physical, mental, emotional, and sexual abuse from Ray.

Michelle would fight Ray all the time to keep him off of Nessa; Nessa would be sobbing and shaking so bad. Ray would threaten them both; Michelle was not scared to protect her sister. "Leave her alone," Michelle yelled intensely. "You're in my house," Ray yelled back. Then, Francis had another surgery. He would always take her to places that he didn't tell her mom. He took her to the train station, but he was supposed to take her to the store. Ray would make her do things that she didn't want to do. She was only a child. Then, he would have the audacity to tell a child not to let a man put his head between her legs. But, he felt comfortable doing what he was doing to a child. He was sick (still is). He would keep a gun on a seat and threaten to kill my mother if I spoke a word.

As a child, Nessa would question her mother's relationship with men and her children constantly in her mind. She was so confused as a child because she was carrying so many things for many years. She still had not recovered from being called a liar. Later, Francis' tiller went missing from her garden. Ray was the only person to use it. They lived on a dead-end street, Hardy Alley St. with just three houses on that street. As Francis was getting back on her feet preparing to go back to work, Ray told Francis that Nessa and Michelle gave her tiller away. The beatings continued and continued. Life was not good as a child. One day, Nessa and Michelle got home from school. Michelle had to step outside and go somewhere; Ray stopped by the house. At the time, he worked for a cab company. Ray came into the house and jumped on top of Nessa in the living room. He tried to kiss her and pull her pants down. Michelle ran into the house and started beating him. She got him off Nessa, and he was so mad.

Later that day, the next-door neighbor told them he saw a big black snake in Ray's garden. He told everyone to be careful. When Francis came home, Ray told her that Nessa didn't wash dishes that day after school. Ray encouraged Francis to make Nessa go pick vegetables out of the garden. It was dark on the dead-end street with one pole light. Nessa was so afraid. She kept thinking to herself, "Why would you send a child to a garden when people have seen a black snake?" Nessa went out to pick the vegetables, crying in fear. Nessa knew God was with her. Years later, they moved out of the house, and Ray did too. People ended up tearing the house down and finding the biggest black snake under the house. It made the news.

When Nessa was in Jr. High, she met a friend at her school named Pam; Nessa knew Pam was more advanced than she was. Pam always wanted to protect her. Because Nessa was so shy and scared in school. Pam lived on the next road behind Ray's house. Nessa spent a lot of time with Pam after Michelle left to go live with her aunt. Nessa was so sad because her sister left. She would talk to Pam on the phone to help her with her sister's departure. Sometimes, she would go across the street in front of Ray's house to write poems. She needed to get away from all the drama in her house. At this point, it was painful. Nessa was never a bad child; she tried to keep the peace. She didn't like to fight or cause trouble. Later, Michelle came back home, and Nessa was so glad. Her life had been hell. One Sunday, Nessa's mother let Nessa and Michelle go with Ray to his cousin's house to get her something. A bomb was dropped; Ray walked into her living room and began talking to a lady, Ann.

Michelle and Nessa followed his cousin to the kitchen where she showed them everything he stole from their mother. She told them that she knew they were getting whoopings for things they were not doing. She said she wanted to tell them because she had cancer, and she was dying. She felt bad because she knew this information. They looked at each other scared to death, and she said Ray is planning on leaving your mother shortly, and the lady in the living room is his ex-girlfriend. They did break up later. They didn't understand why she was telling them that.

Later, Nessa's grandmother, Linda, moved in with them. Nessa was so glad because she loved her grandmother, and she told her everything. She did everything she could to help her. Nessa asked her mother if she could go over to Pam's house to go with her to see her grandmother. Francis said it was okay, but she had to be home by midnight. Nessa said, ok. Ray slowed down in his interaction with them. After Nessa got to Pam's house, Pam's mother encouraged them to let Pam's boyfriend and his brother take them. Nessa felt something was wrong, but she still got in the car. Later, Nessa realized they were heading to Charlotte, and she wanted to know where they were going. Pam said to the airport to watch planes. Nessa was disappointed because they didn't tell her mother about going to the airport. Then, Nessa reminded Pam that they had to be home at midnight, and Pam said ok. Nessa was so scared, and she realized that Pam used her. Pam's friend's brother was trying to talk to Nessa, but Nessa told him she didn't want a boyfriend. She was too young at the time, only 14. Pam asked them to get out of the car for 30 minutes, so Nessa and the other guy watched planes and talked. They got Nessa home at 12:15; Nessa knew she was going to get a beating for being late.

When Nessa got to the door, Michelle told her she had just gotten a beating because she was late. As soon as Francis saw Nessa, she started beating her everywhere with a belt so bad. Nessa wanted to die. It got worse when Francis made her pull her pants down in front of her boyfriend. Ray was standing at the door with a smile, a sexual look on his face, and his tongue hanging out. Francis continued to beat her and say horrible things to her. She continued to call her worthless and stupid. No mother should ever say those things to her daughter or child period. Nessa screamed out, " Why don't you kill me?" Nessa was so tired of the beatings and everything she had been through. She didn't want to live anymore. Francis got a knife from the kitchen and put the knife at Nessa's throat. At that time, Nessa's grandmother was ill and confused, but she called her daughter's name out loud. "STOP, THAT IS ENOUGH." Her mother had enough sense to know she was wrong and stopped. She knew she had gone too far.

Nessa's grandmother lost her mind. Nessa's mother, Francis, had been through a difficult childhood because her mother was not stable mentally. Francis had to take care of her siblings. Nessa realized her mother went through a bad ordeal. She doesn't know what changed her mother. Was it the result of her childhood or was it when she met Ray? She will never know, but the love for her mother will never change. Nessa had to forgive everyone who abused her. She knows she serves a forgiving God. The little girl within her is being set free.

She wrote this book to free every little girl or woman who has been a victim of mental, emotional, and sexual abuse. This is for the girl or woman who has dealt with sexual assault and rape at the hands of your mother's boyfriends, boyfriends, daddies, uncles, or any other predators.

CHAPTER 2

Damaged, but Not Broken

Good

Bad

& UGLY

As a young girl, Nessa loved the church and singing in the choir. She was the lead soloist, and she worked in the youth and missionary departments. Her mother kept her busy working in the church. She loved to be in the church. Life was great until that dark cloud entered her mother's life. Francis listened to Ray, so Nessa had no choice but to suffer. When they moved to their new home, Francis and Ray were broken up. Although they were broken up, it did not stop the damage that had already happened. Nessa's life had changed. She wasn't the same little girl anymore. Her self-esteem was low, and she didn't care about anything anymore. She started to experience bullying in school. " You are not smart. Why is your hair so short." She still remembers the remarks. Kids would eat off of her plate, and she didn't tell anyone. She still remembers a girl yelling in her face while she was waiting for her sister to walk her home: " I am going to beat you up." Michelle always came to the rescue to tell the kids to leave her alone. She couldn't talk to her mother because of the past experiences she had just come out of. She was in a closet, and she didn't know how to come out of it. At the age of 15, she would go to church with some of her older friends and pray for an answer. She was still lost. Her mother would let her older friends have bible study at their new house.

Six months passed and Francis told Nessa about their next-door neighbors and their family. They were always very nice to Nessa's family. After they got settled in their new home, the neighbors invited Nessa and friends over. Francis let her go. The older crowd was playing cards, and the young people were playing games. Everybody was drinking, but she did not tell her mother. There was an older guy at the house. He wanted to know Nessa's name. She told him her name. He looked at her and said, " You are a pretty young girl with a beautiful shape. She smiled and thought he was handsome. She told him that she was 15. He told her that his name was Paul. When she went over the next day, the neighbor told her that Paul liked her. The neighbor said that she told Paul she was too young, but he gave me this gift to give you. Nessa smiled, it was a beautiful necklace with his aunt's phone number on a piece of paper. Nessa was looking for love. Two weeks later, her mother let her go back to the house. She was happy because this time she really liked Paul. She was planning to let him know. When she got over there, he was glad to see her. He kissed her on the jaw. She told Paul that her birthday was coming soon. He asked the lady of the house if he could talk to Nessa in private. She told him he could take her in the den and shut the door. Behind closed doors, he started to manipulate her. He told her how much he loved her and started kissing her. He told her he would protect her and make her feel good. He started to remove her panties and underwear. Then, he kissed her private part. For some reason, she trusted him but didn't fully know what was going on. She knew it felt good. After it was over, Nessa told him she had to go home. He asked her if she felt good. She told Paul, "yes." He called Nessa later that day. She was so shy about what happened. He told her that it was love. When Nessa turned 16, Francis let Paul sit in her living room every other weekend for two hours.

Unfortunately, Francis and Ray got back together. Nessa was sad. During the season of Francis and Ray reuniting, Nessa met her father; he was drunk. She was hurt, and she started drinking silently. Some of her older friends that she grew up with at her home church, Wayside in Gastonia, would pick her up and take her to revival. The pastor was Rev. T.M. Walker. Nessa would tell them that she just wanted to be free from the bad things that happened to her. She can remember her mother letting them have Bible Study at her house. The Bible Study sessions encouraged her to pursue a relationship with her father. Nessa started to go to Charlotte to see her father. At her father's house, she could drink and do whatever she wanted to. She knew it wasn't right, but she wanted to be close to her dad. While at her father's house, she would contact Paul. Paul told her that he missed her, but she was upset with him because he lied about so many things. At this stage in Nessa's life, she was lost. She was upset with her mom for taking Ray back. She started to make terrible decisions, and she did not care about them. One night, she went out with an older friend, but her mother told her not to go. And, her friend ended up getting them kidnapped (must write another book).

When Nessa turned 17, her mother let Paul take her out one night. She had to be home by 12:30. Paul told Nessa he wanted to get something to eat and get a hotel room. He told her they didn't have to do anything; he just wanted to be alone with her. Later, he wanted her to let him put the head in. He said nothing would happen. She told him this was her first time. She was scared, but she let him put the head in. He forgot and got excited. She started to bleed like crazy. Nessa was crying and feeling so shameful. All he could say was that I feel okay now. Nessa told him to take her home. The next day, he gave her a ring. Nessa was so confused about how she was feeling. A few weeks later, Nessa started to get sick. She found out she was pregnant and her mother beat her. Paul already had two kids he had to take care of, but he lied about so much of his life. She was left with scars and pain. Through all the hurt, God still had a plan.

CHAPTER 3

Poems From the Heart

I dream of my everlasting home beyond the twilight zone.
A home made of light gold stone.
A place where I belong,
No more sorrow, no more pain, abundant life I will gain.
Peace and happiness all the time
What a great joy divine!

Someone to Watch Over Me

Jesus watches over me from day to day.
He teaches me what to say.
He watches me as I kneel and pray,
And through the night as I lay.
Jesus is a friend of mine.
He was there all the time.
A friend like him is hard to find.
He is just one of a kind.

CHAPTER 4

In the Midst of Life's storms

Nessa looked over her life and reflected on her many stories. She remembers when she was 26 years old with two kids. She was so tired of putting up with her cheating boyfriend. Women were calling her house all hours of the day and night telling her about her man. They didn't understand why she was still with him. They had no idea that she was trying to get out, but she was scared of him. She didn't want to hurt her kids, but she was so unhappy. She knew these were the consequences of not being in the will of God. Sin....Sin.... Sin... was the blame.

There was a day that Nessa remembered like it was yesterday. She was off work, and she had put her kids down for a nap. That night, she had cried all night long; she tried her best to hide her feelings from her kids. She knew it was time to let him go; she just couldn't handle the abuse anymore. She called her mother telling her she didn't want to live anymore, and she wanted her to take care of her kids. Her mother cried and told her not to do anything. Nessa hung up the phone, and she immediately went to the bathroom. She got the pill out of the cabinet, and she put the pill in her hands. She was getting ready to take the pills when she heard a voice say her name three times. She looked around, and there was no one. The voice got louder and said her name three times. She started crying. She ran into the room to make sure her kids were still sleeping. When she returned to the bathroom, she looked in the mirror. The voice said, "Don't give your life up for no one but me." I started crying harder. Then, there was a loud hit on the door. It was the police and the ambulance. Nessa told them that she was okay. She was feeling better, but she was upset with her mother. She didn't expect her to call considering all the years she suffered as a child.

When her boyfriend called, she told him it was over. Immediately, she got on one knee and asked God to forgive and help her. The next day, she went downtown to put her kids' father on child support. Paul put her through so much and persuaded her son to move in with him. Nessa decided to get back to church for a while. Shortly, she gave up hope again and started living any kind of way. She was mad at the world. She started dating bad guys; she was very angry.

Summer of 2000.......................Changed Nessa's life again

.....................Another Betrayal.......................

Nessa met a new guy named Ron; they worked at the Main Airlines at the Douglas Airport in Charlotte. He was a very quiet guy and well known. They laughed and enjoyed their jobs together even though they had only been there for a few months. Ron informed Nessa that he liked her and would like to know her better. She liked Ron, but her past kept her withdrawn and quiet. After some time, she agreed to see Ron outside of the job because he was such a gentleman. Ron was a very private person, and she liked that about him. She did not want anyone to know they were seeing each other, so they decided to keep their friendship a secret. They continued to see each other, and he showered her with gifts. She couldn't help but think that he wanted more. Nessa informed him that she would continue to see him, but sex was not an option. She wanted to wait until they had built a strong relationship. His personality didn't change; he continued to talk with his friends, clowning around and discussing sports. He loved to have fun on his job. He continued to give Nessa anything he thought she needed or asked for. Although Nessa had feelings for Ron, there was another friend she liked too. The only problem was that her friend, Alex, was married. Ron was aware that Nessa's heart was with this married friend; she admired him a lot, and he was her confidant and safety net. She could not move on from him. Nessa explained to Ron that Alex had been there for her when she was in a low place. She knew she would never have Alex, and she was trying to walk away. He had been so good to her. Ron told her that if their relationship became permanent she could no longer be friends with Alex.

Nessa talked to Alex and told him she had met a nice single gentleman on her job that she would like to pursue. Alex didn't like it, but he told Nessa that he would always be there for her. He loved her, and he walked away. After her separation from Alex, her car broke down. Ron came and picked her up for three days while her car was in the shop. He paid for her car to get fixed. A month later, Nessa's car started back up. She put her car in the shop for five days this time. Ron allowed her to drive his new BMW because her car needed repairs. Ron had two cars, a BMW and an old beat-up car. He drove his old car. Nessa began to let her guard down and felt she must be special for him to allow her to drive his new car while denying himself.

Ron has been to Nessa's house a few times, but Nessa had no interest in going to his house. He told her a big football game was scheduled for Sunday, and they were both off work. He invited her over to his house to watch the game with him. Nessa's car had been repaired, so she agreed to go over to his house and watch the game. He was planning to cook for her. Nessa arrived at 4:00 pm, and the game was scheduled to start at 6 pm allowing them time to eat dinner first. Since this was the first time she had been to his condo, she was nervous. She liked to be at the house; it was the only place she felt safe. She could smell the food cooking in the kitchen when she arrived. He made her feel very welcome. His condo was very clean with his living room abiding all white with a fluffy white carpet. His bathroom and bedroom were all white. They smelled fresh. After the tour through his house, she put her shoes at the door. Then, a bad feeling came over her. She couldn't understand why. He had always treated her so well.

Nessa sat down on the floor; then, Ron came from the kitchen with two glasses of red wine. He began to drink the wine and offered Nessa a glass. She took a sip; she was okay. She sipped again and started talking to Ron. She started to drink the wine. Shortly afterward, she attempted to have a conversation with him, but she was not feeling well. She remembered hearing music playing in the background and the room started spinning. She could not get up off the floor. Ron asked her to dance with him, and he started kissing her and dancing with her. Nessa was so out of it mentally. She heard another man's voice in the background; then, everything went black Upon waking up the next morning, Nessa had the worst headache you could imagine. She was unable to hold her head up; it was hurting so badly. Nessa felt like a train had hit her; she did not feel well at all. Her stomach was hurting and sore all over. It hurt to even move. Nessa had never felt like this before. Nessa was naked in his bed; she was numb with a pounding headace.

The room looked like a storm had just come through it. It was hard to believe after being so lovely during the initial tour. Ron was sleeping with a condom still on his penis. She looked at the time; it was 10:00 am. Ron woke to find Nessa crying in disbelief. "Why? Why? Why? Is this happening to me," she yelled at Ron. There was so much going through Nessa's mind. Why was her body in so much pain and sore? Nessa yelled at Ron saying," I did not come to your house for you to rape me!!!" He responded, "No, we made love." Nessa shouted, "We did not make love, and I can not remember anything." Nessa asked God to please make her understand what happened. Her clothes were all over the room along with his. As Nessa was trying to get her clothes on, she was hurting and in so much pain. She cried out uncontrollably. She told Ron not to say a word to her, and she rushed to get her clothes.

She got her key and started walking slowly to the door. She was sick to her stomach. Ron jumped up and said the sex was great. Nessa never said a word; she kept walking to the door. She was crying as she walked to her car. She drove home slowly; her body was aching with pain. When she got home, the phone was ringing. It was Ron. She told him to never call her again unless it was job-related. She wanted to die; her heart was racing. She called her job and told them she was sick and coming down with something. Nessa got in the shower; it felt like she was in there for three hours crying. She was angry at the world. She was disappointed in the world and disappointed in herself. She thought she was losing her mind. After she scrubbed herself down in the shower, the incident took her back to her childhood hearing her mother's boyfriend say, "no one would believe her; everyone knows she is a liar." She started to question herself: "Why has this happened to me?" I will never trust again; I am damaged goods. Nessa was so disappointed with her life. She could not tell her mother at the time. The only person she could think to call was her married friend, Alex. She needed him now. Nessa called her friend Alex on the cell phone and asked him to come over. She cried out to him, telling him that she needed him now. He told her that he was on the way.

When Alex arrived, he found Nessa wearing a bathrobe, wet, shaking, and crying out of control. She first told him that she was sorry for hurting him. Then, she told him what happened to her again. He asked her to calm down, so he can better understand her. Before this happened, Alex had encouraged Nessa to go to counseling to deal with abuse. Nessa told him that she believed she had been date-raped and another person was involved. As the fog began to clear, she remembered being dizzy. She heard two voices talking. Alex was steaming hot and upset; he began fussing and cussing. He wanted to know his name and where he lived. Nessa did not tell him because Alex always had a gun in his car. Nessa told him that they worked together. Nessa told Alex that he said that they made love, but she was hurt and sore all over. He told her to call the hospital triage nurse; she did. After Nessa told the nurse everything, she informed her that she had been date raped and to come in. Nessa was informed not to take a shower, but Nessa had already taken one. Nessa hung up the phone and told Alex that they are not going to believe her because she went to his house. Alex said that he didn't care because he did not have the right to do this. Nessa began to cry because she knew no one would believe her. She started crying harder. Nessa was ashamed because she didn't want her story to be publicized. She was still dealing with the pain from the past.

Alex was so sad for her because he truly loved Nessa in his own way. Nessa cried harder. Alex had always been there for Nessa; he called Nessa's counselor to get her some help. Nessa remembered seeing Alex on her couch crying because he felt helpless. Nessa soaked three times a day. Alex was an older gentleman, and he used some of his mother's old-time remedies to nurse Nessa back to health. Alex held her as she slept for three nights. As she slept, she had nightmares from her past that haunted her; she took five days off from work. When she went back to work, Ron kept lying about that night every time he saw Nessa at work. Nessa transferred to Raleigh. For years, she blamed herself. She made Alex swear he would never tell anyone. Alex always said that he hated that he wasn't there to protect her. She reminded him not to tell anyone, and he never did. Nessa never knew what Alex told his wife. Alex directed Nessa to the right people to assist her and get her life back on track. He took this secret to his grave.

Years later, Alex called Nessa when she got back in town and told her he had cancer. His cancer had come back after twenty years, and it was terminal. Nessa was so sad. He told her that they needed to ask God for forgiveness, and they did. Nessa wrote his wife a letter asking her to forgive her for being with her husband. She told her she was sorry, and she was wrong. Nessa told her she was lost and needed help.

RIP, Alex 09/20/2007

CHAPTER 5

A Lonely Cry

Life has had its ups and downs for Nessa; she realized how life can change in a split second. After a day of work, Nessa flew back to Gastonia after working in Raleigh, NC from US AIRWAYS where she was stationed. She still lived in Gastonia, and she needed to make a doctor's appointment for the next day because she noticed a red rash on her swollen face. She had just gotten off of penicillin from an allergic reaction.

Then, her doctor put her back on penicillin and took her out of work. He gave her pain pills, so she could relax. She wasn't feeling good. Three days later, Nessa realized her condition was getting worse, not better. She called her doctor; they told her to let the medicine take its course. Nessa was ashamed of how her face looked. At that time, she didn't have any visitors other than her daughter, best friend, and one of her brothers occasionally. Her brother had his own problems. Nessa had no idea she would be out of work that long. After she was out of PTO hours and waiting on her disability check, Nessa and her daughter, Tonya, had to do without until her best friend got her food and tires for her car. Her mother made sure they ate one time a day. Nessa believes it was because her daughter lived with her. Nessa's son never came over to her house because he lived with his father. Nessa had so much bitterness in her heart. Nessa held the dark secret to protect her mother, Francis. Her mother didn't protect her, and the tables got turned. Nessa wanted to die.

How is it that the people you love the most can hurt you the worst? Her other siblings didn't know her pain, but her older sister, Michelle, knew about her childhood trauma. Nessa was crying in front of her daughter one day. "They are calling me a liar," Nessa yelled. Tonya said, "Mom, I know you are telling the truth." Nessa flipped out and ran over to her mother and stepfather's house. She knocked on the door, and they would not open it. Nessa's mother used to babysit her daughter a lot while Nessa worked two jobs. She always told her to keep her daughter close to her. Nessa knew something was wrong. She told the family secret, and her family was mad at her. They were not talking to her.

The next night, Nessa was moaning and groaning. She looked up at the door, and her daughter, Tonya, was crying. Nessa was tired of her family and being called a liar, but she knew the truth. Later on, Nessa started breathing heavily. Tonya ran over to her grandmother's house and told them. Francis said, "This is what happens when you do people wrong. " Nessa said that she will never forget it, but she is too weak and out of breath. She needs help and must go to the hospital. At this point, Nessa wanted to give up. As she watched her daughter cry and have the hurt in her face, she knew she had to keep fighting. Nessa was dying on the inside, and she had already been through so much.

Nessa passed out in the ER; they said she was dehydrated. After leaving the hospital, Nessa still didn't feel well. She took a nap. Then, she woke up and drove herself and Tonya to Presbyterian in Charlotte. They checked Nessa out; people were laughing at Nessa's swollen face. Her face looked bad; Nessa's daughter was getting upset. Nessa said, "it's ok." Then, they went home. Nessa started having a hard time breathing. Nessa called Tonya's father to come over to her house to stay the night. If she died that night, she didn't want her daughter to be alone. Nessa's daughter did not have a good night's sleep in such a long time. Tonya went to sleep since her father was there. Nessa waited for everyone to fall asleep; then, she cried out to God. She asked God to forgive her, and she repented from her sins. She asked to take all the hate and unforgiveness away. She wanted him to help her renew her faith and forgive everyone who has hurt and abused her. She repeated the sinner's prayer and fell asleep. For the first time in a long time, Nessa had a great, relaxed night. She went back to her primary care office the next day. Her doctor wasn't there, so she saw the Nurse Practitioner; she checked Nessa out. She immediately took her off of penicillin and started her on a new medicine. The next day, her swelling went down. Nessa was feeling better. The nurse practitioner told her she could never take penicillin anymore because it would kill her. Then, Nessa started going back to counseling for all of her abuse and got the help she needed. God turned her life around for the better............................. THANK YOU JESUS

CHAPTER 6

Testimonies and Praise Reports

Nessa has many testimonies. In 2008, she had a tumor removed. The doctor told her that she had a 30 percent chance to live, but God was on her side. She lost a portion of her small intestines, and she had a bowel obstruction. In 2009, six months later, she had a hernia repaired with mesh surgery. In 2011, Mesh damaged her gallbladder. She was told that she would be on medicine for the rest of her life. She went to have gallbladder surgery with a laparoscopic incision. After they put her to sleep, they realized they couldn't do surgery because of the mesh. Then, the next month; In 2012, they did the large incision. She had to go to the office three times to get my stomach checked. Nessa's daughter, god-brother, and son's girlfriend had to watch doctors save her life because her intestines were having some difficulties. The doctors were forced to do an emergency procedure right in his office. The doctor told Nessa that she would only have a year to live after removing the tumor because it was in a bad spot. God has been good to Nessa. After 14 years, she is still standing.

With every testimony comes a praise report! On Nessa's birthday, August 9th, 2017, she was diagnosed with an esophagus ring and chronic stomach disease. The doctors told her that she could lose her life. She was told that nothing could grow in that spot. Chemo and radiation would not do me any good. After her procedure on August 9th, they found Helicobacter pylori growing in her small intestines. The doctor called her with two bad reports on her special day. After all the tests, biopsies, and treatments, Nessa is still alive. Through all the tears, prayers, and fasting, her faith never wavered. She knew greater was coming; she had something better than money. She had God's favor over her life. Her tests came back, and everything was normal. The doctors were amazed. Before she could tell the nurses God favored her, they already said it. They did the test twice to make sure. She told them that she was healed in Jesus' name. God handpicked Nessa because He knew she would trust Him through every trial. Nessa is highly favored. She is dedicated to giving God the praise he deserves and the honor. She is in it to win it. God has plans for Nessa.

CHAPTER 7

A Fresh Start

Nessa faced a lot of emotional and physical abuse in her childhood, teenage, and adult years. She had to learn to gather the pieces of her life; she didn't know how to put herself back together. When she was a teenager, she started writing poems daily to ease her pain. Her most memorable poem was " I Dream of an Everlasting Home Beyond the Twilight Zone" mentioned in Chapter 3. She wrote about how she felt, and her desire to go to heaven. Surely, life in heaven had to be better than what she was experiencing on earth. When she sang in the choir, she would lead one of her favorite songs, "Jesus is Coming." She would also reflect on her favorite scripture, Psalms 147:3 (NIV): "He heals the brokenhearted and binds up their wounds." This scripture helped her to no longer be a victim of her past.

Nessa had to realize she had to let go of her past to be free and have forgiveness in her heart. For years and years, she went back and forth until one day Nessa was watching the film, *Woman thou art Loosed*. She cried and cried; then, a couple of years later she was watching *War Room*. She felt God so heavy in those two movies, and she realized she needed to be healed. One day, she cleaned her hallway closet and made her own war room. She started to pray and fast three times a day; fasting caused her to deny the things she loved the most such as food and television. She only wanted to seek God's face and hear from heaven.

Then, God started moving in her life like never before. She heard so many people and family members with negative comments about her, but she didn't stop waiting on the Lord. She let go of her male friends. She just wanted to be free. She began to tell God about everybody who hurt and abused her. She cried out to the Lord for help to take the shame away from her bad decisions. She just wanted to be whole. She knew God was aware of all the pain, but she wanted to pour out her pain to Him. She knew people would say she was crazy for airing her dirty laundry. Nessa knew it was a part of the process.

Nessa believed her book would help a lot of people deal with past issues that had a very hard time moving forward. Wow, it took her over 30+ years to release the shame from her past. She was worried about family and people; she realized her feelings were keeping her in bondage. When people violate others at their most vulnerable moments, they can become afraid to tell because they have been told not to. One will become bitter and unforgiving. Nessa is no longer bitter, and she knows her story is necessary. God has been so good to her. She is excited about the plan He has for her life. God has given me a second chance at life. No matter what has happened, God wants us to make him our solid foundation and our source.

On Sunday, May 5th, 2019, she was re-baptized. While she was on her way to church, she was singing in the car. When she got on the highway, she heard a loud noise. After pulling her car over on the side of the road, she noticed she had a flat tire. She called her daughter to pick her up; she didn't want to be late. My best friend didn't get to see me get baptized because my daughter was going to pick her up. Her car was in the shop. But, I knew her prayers were with me.

She was very young when she first got baptized, so this baptism was very important. On that Sunday morning, she fell to her knees praying to God. She didn't want to carry the burdens any longer. She needed a fresh start, and she thanked Him for loving and forgiving her. As the tears rolled down her face, she started seeing doors open. When she went down in the water, He removed all her shame and gave her back her esteem. As she cast her burdens on him, she realized how much he cared for her. When she came out of the water with tears in her eyes, she would never be the same again. God gave her a sense of direction to face life's journey. No matter how hard times get, she knows she can depend on Him for everything. He will meet my needs. Sometimes, we will lose people along the way. Don't lose your focus.

Nessa's prayer was simple:

"Thank you, Father, for opening up my eyes and heart to hear your voice and be willing to forgive everyone that ever hurt me. I will love them the way God loved us. I will pray that people will change their lives before it is too late. I am a winner............................ I have been set free. I must release the bitterness and hate and exchange it for love and peace. God will handle the rest. Never let people make you feel bad about your mistakes or tell the truth because he or she has his or her demons to deal with. Pride will keep one from changing, and he or she can't let pride win.

She leaves her readers with a scripture of encouragement to keep living:

Romans 14:11 (NIV) "For it has been written...... I live saith the Lord, every knee shall bow to me and every tongue shall confess to God.

About the Author

LaDonna Smith is a God - Fearing down to earth Christian Lady. Her focus is to empower her readers through the power of prayers and forgiveness; your life will never be the same again. She resides in Charlotte, North Carolina, with two adult children Son and daughter, and an amazing granddaughter. Her goal is to be a motivational speaker.

For Bookings visit www.Ladonnadsmith.com

In memory of Jason McLean.

Thank you for encouraging and loving me without judgement.

www.ingramcontent.com/pod-product-compliance
Lightning Source LLC
Chambersburg PA
CBHW031227090426
42740CB00007B/739